J 333.7071 ROS
Rose, Simon, 1961– author.
Evaluating arguments about the
environment

State Your Case

Evaluating Arguments About
Environment

Simon Rose

CRABTREE
PUBLISHING COMPANY
WWW.CRABTREEBOOKS.COM

Author: Simon Rose
Series research and development: Reagan Miller
Editors: Sarah Eason, Claudia Martin, Jennifer Sanderson, and Janine Deschenes
Proofreaders: Tracey Kelly, Wendy Scavuzzo
Indexer: Tracey Kelly
Editorial director: Kathy Middleton
Design: Paul Myerscough and Steve Mead
Cover design: Katherine Berti
Photo research: Claudia Martin
Production coordinator and Prepress technician: Katherine Berti
Print coordinator: Katherine Berti

Produced for Crabtree Publishing Company by Calcium Creative Ltd

Photo Credits:
t=Top, c=Center, b=Bottom, l=Left, r=Right.

Inside: Shutterstock: Air Images: p.18; Albert Karimov: p.33; ArtOfPhotos: p.34; Darren Baker: p.28; Dawna Moore: p.42; Dirk Ercken: p.27; Dmitri Ma: p.29; elwynn: p.4; Fotokon: p.10; Frontpage: pp.20, 21; Grischa Georgiew: pp.36–7; Have a nice day Photo: p.37; jayjune69: p.6; JaySi: p.30; Jordi C: p.15; Katesalin Pagkaihang: pp.1, 24; Kutikan: p.25; Linda Parton: p.31; Marten_House: p.39; MIA Studio: p.23; Monkey Business Images: pp.8, 16, 41; Nokuru: pp.3, 35; otnaydur: p.11; Ovknhr: p.19; Photographee.eu: p.14; PixieMe: p.26; Pressmaster; p.32; Protasov: p.9; Rich Carey: p.17; Sirisak_baokaew: p.22; Syda Productions: pp.40, 43; Vasily Gureev: p.5; vchal: p.7; Vladimir Kogan Michael: p.12; wavebreakmedia: p.38; XXLPhoto: p.13.

Cover: Shutterstock: Trong Nguyen (l); Rich Carey (r)
All other images from Shutterstock

Library and Archives Canada Cataloguing in Publication

Rose, Simon, 1961-, author
    Evaluating arguments about the environment / Simon Rose.

(State your case)
Includes bibliographical references and index.
Issued in print and electronic formats.
ISBN 978-0-7787-5080-2 (hardcover).--
ISBN 978-0-7787-5105-2 (softcover).--
ISBN 978-1-4271-2165-3 (HTML)

    1. Environmental ethics--Juvenile literature.   2. Environmental protection--Moral and ethical aspects--Juvenile literature.
3. Environmental protection--Juvenile literature.   4. Critical thinking--Juvenile literature.   5. Thought and thinking--Juvenile literature.
6. Reasoning--Juvenile literature.   7. Persuasion (Rhetoric)--Juvenile literature.   I. Title.

GE42.R67 2018   j179'.1   C2018-903035-6
                                              C2018-903036-4

Library of Congress Cataloging-in-Publication Data

CIP available at the Library of Congress

Crabtree Publishing Company
www.crabtreebooks.com   1-800-387-7650

Printed in the U.S.A./092018/CG20180810

Copyright © **2019 CRABTREE PUBLISHING COMPANY**. All rights reserved. No part of this publication may be reproduced, stored in a retrieval system, or be transmitted in any form or by any means, electronic, mechanical, photocopying, recording, or otherwise, without the prior written permission of Crabtree Publishing Company. In Canada: We acknowledge the financial support of the Government of Canada through the Canada Book Fund for our publishing activities.

Published in Canada
Crabtree Publishing
616 Welland Ave.
St. Catharines, Ontario
L2M 5V6

Published in the United States
Crabtree Publishing
PMB 59051
350 Fifth Avenue, 59th Floor
New York, New York 10118

Published in the United Kingdom
Crabtree Publishing
Maritime House
Basin Road North, Hove
BN41 1WR

Published in Australia
Crabtree Publishing
3 Charles Street
Coburg North
VIC, 3058

CONTENTS

Chapter 1
The Environment Today and Tomorrow   4

Chapter 2
What Makes an Argument?   8

Chapter 3
Should Clear-Cutting Forests for Agriculture Be Allowed?   20

Chapter 4
Does Bottled Water Do More Harm Than Good?   28

Chapter 5
Should Schools Go Paperless?   36

Bibliography   44
Glossary   46
Learning More   47
Index and About the Author   48

CHAPTER 1
THE ENVIRONMENT TODAY AND TOMORROW

Human beings have built amazing cities, factories, vehicles, and computers. We have made both negative and positive impacts on our environment in the process. We all depend on the environment for clean water, fresh air, and enough food to eat. It makes sense to protect Earth for ourselves and for future **generations**.

Most people agree that protecting the environment is very important, both now and in the future. However, not everyone agrees on the best way to do so. It has been difficult to think of the ways humans can continue to invent, travel, and build while still protecting the planet. Today, Earth is threatened in many different ways. There are problems with land, air, and water pollution, **deforestation**, a lack of fresh water, and extreme weather. The planet's population also continues to grow every year. In 1900, the world's population was 1.6 billion, and in 2018 it was 7.6 billion. This growth means that every year, there are even more people using more and more of the planet's **resources**.

Pollution from vehicles creates fumes in towns and cities that cause health problems for people and sometimes reduce visibility.

Problems with Waste

A main issue faced by humankind is what we should do with all the waste we create in all aspects of our lives—from the food packaging we throw out at home to the waste that **industries** such as farming create to produce goods. In most countries, people recycle some materials, such as metals from cans, glass from bottles, paper from newspapers, and some plastics from packaging. Some items that cannot currently be recycled are **incinerated**, or burned. However, many items still end up in giant **landfills**. Some items, such as batteries, electronics, and paint, are harmful when they end up in landfills because substances from them can seep into the ground and cause health problems in plants and animals. Today, there is much research into improving recycling methods, particularly for plastics. There is also research into producing **bioplastics**, which are plastics made from easily recyclable plant materials.

Hydroelectric power is a renewable energy source. However, to harness the power, we must build dams and power lines, both of which damage the environment.

Deforestation

Some of the foods we eat and products we use every day may be grown on farms that have been created by cutting down forests. In **tropical** regions (areas near the equator, an imaginary line around the center of Earth), farmers often create more farmland by cutting down trees. Crops grown on such land include tea, coffee, rice, rubber, soybeans, and palm oil. Soybeans are used to make bread, cooking oils, desserts, paint, and **fertilizer**. Palm oil is used in ice cream, margarine, shower gels, **detergents**, and **cosmetics**. Products made from trees themselves include paper, timber for houses, and wooden furniture, utensils, sports equipment, and musical instruments. In North America, however, many wooden items are today made from trees taken from **managed forests**, where the number of trees cut down and the number of new trees planted are strictly controlled.

Despite efforts to slow deforestation, such as forest management, it is estimated that continuing to cut down trees at the current rate will cause the world's tropical forests to disappear in fewer than 100 years. All forests, and tropical forests in particular, are home to a vast range of birds, mammals, reptiles, amphibians, insects, and spiders. Increasing numbers of species that live in tropical forests, such as the Amazon, are **endangered**. Deforestation could push some animals into **extinction**.

The Issue of Fossil Fuels

For a long time, people have relied on **fossil fuels**—coal, oil, and natural gas—to supply energy for our homes, cars, and industries. Fossil fuels are not a **renewable** source of energy because someday they will run out. In addition, a major environmental problem with fossil fuels is that they contribute to **global warming**. When they are burned, fossil fuels give off the gas carbon dioxide, which traps heat in Earth's **atmosphere**. Today, many countries are investing large sums of money in harnessing cleaner, renewable sources of energy, such as solar, water, and wind power. More controversially, some are looking into **nuclear power**, which is power generated by a nuclear reaction. Many car manufacturers are developing cars that run on electric batteries rather than gas. Perhaps, one day soon, our reliance on fossil fuels will be a thing of the past.

THE ENVIRONMENT TODAY AND TOMORROW

Hot Topics?

It is likely that you have heard many people express their opinions about the issues facing the environment on Earth. For example, many people think humans generate too much plastic waste and debate whether we need tougher laws about plastics. Some people wonder if recycling is working or whether incineration should be used more often to capture the energy that is released in the process. There is also the issue of whether humans are able to continue to live in larger and larger cities while still protecting Earth.

Arguing About the Environment

People make arguments that present their opinions about environmental issues on the news, in opinion blogs and articles, and in regular conversation. You need to be able to work through the arguments to decide which ones are **credible**—and which are not. That way, you can start to form your own opinions about the environment and how the issues affect you.

In this book, we'll take a look at some arguments about environmental issues. We'll look at the features of an argument, what makes a strong argument, and how to decide if you agree with it or not. Let's start by taking a look at the argument on the opposite page, which is about whether or not humans **generate**, or make, too much waste.

As cities increase in size, the people who live there use more power and generate more waste. As a result, more resources are used and more landfills are built.

Do You Agree?

"Do humans generate too much waste?"

HUMANS GENERATE TOO MUCH WASTE.

We waste food by leaving it uneaten, and have excessively large packaging on many of the products we buy. We have **junk mail** delivered to our homes, which is thrown straight in the trash. Electronic gadgets wear out within a few years and have to be disposed of. The batteries these devices contain may leak deadly **mercury** into the soil. They are made from materials that do not naturally break down in the environment. Plastics take hundreds of years to **decompose**, or rot, so car tires and bottles just pile up in landfills.

A 2013 report by the World Bank stated that the world's solid waste will increase from 3.5 to 6 million tons (3.1 to 5.4 million metric tons) every day by 2025. The United States generated 254 million tons (230 million metric tons) of waste in 2013. "There is no end in sight to this trend," says a spokesperson for the United Nations Environment Programme. The world's population is increasing. As more people are born and cities expand, we will create even more waste. The waste management systems we have in place, such as recycling systems, cannot keep up.

HUMANS DO NOT GENERATE TOO MUCH WASTE.

Humans may have generated too much waste in the past, but today, we are becoming more responsible. Most people are aware of how waste can damage the environment, so they recycle, reuse, and compost many more products. In the United States, 64 percent of paper and cardboard is now recycled. The use of computers has made us less wasteful with paper. Computers and other electronics are now more widely recycled. In 2014, around 42 percent of electronic waste was recycled in the United States. This increased from just 10 percent in 2010. In Canada, electronic recycling increased from 13,000 tons (11,793 metric tons) in 2006 to 92,000 tons (83,461) in 2014.

Waste is also converted into energy, making it useful. In the United States, trash is burned to produce energy. The heat created when waste is burned makes steam, which can be used to heat buildings or turn **turbines** to generate electricity. In 2015, 71 waste-to-energy power plants in the United States generated 14 billion **kilowatt hours** of electricity, enough to power 1,240,000 average U.S. homes for a year. Some landfills also generate electricity using **methane gas** produced from decomposing waste. In Canada in 2014, 8.7 million kilowatt hours of electricity were generated from solid waste.

After reading the arguments about waste, decide which side you agree with. How did you make your choice? Did you rely on personal experience? Does the way the arguments are presented influence your decision?

There are around 2,000 landfill sites in the United States. The average American throws away a staggering 4.4 pounds (2 kg) of trash every day.

CHAPTER 2
WHAT MAKES AN ARGUMENT?

*People have differing opinions about issues. A good argument needs **evidence** to support it and to persuade others of its **validity**.*

An argument is a set of reasons that prove that a person's belief or position on an issue is valid, or correct. Reasons are based on **logic**. Arguments are used to try to change another person's point of view or to persuade them to accept a new point of view. Arguments can also be used to draw support or promote action for a cause.

You read, hear, and see arguments every day. For example, you might see news reporters arguing on the benefits or negative effects of a dam being built. Does the electricity it will create make it worth the possible damage it would do to the ecosystem? You might hear people discussing the benefits of electric cars—one person might think these types of vehicles are great ways to reduce fossil fuel usage, and the other might say they are not practical since there are so few recharging stations. Each person states their ideas, gives their reasons, and, if the argument is strong, supports their reasons with evidence to try to persuade the other person that their ideas are best.

Why Argue?

Arguments have different purposes. Sometimes an argument can help people learn about an issue. It might explain one or both sides of an issue so people can make an informed decision about what they believe. For example, it might explain the advantages and disadvantages of solar power.

Other arguments are persuasive arguments, which try to convince people to agree with certain beliefs or positions. Some of these arguments are used to gather support for a cause, such as restricting or banning the use of chemicals that harm bees, since bees are very important to **ecosystems**. This type of argument is meant to influence the way you think about something, or to change your mind about an issue.

Other arguments are used to solve problems and make decisions. For example, members of a school community might decide to present arguments about whether to give money to support the school's recycling program or to plant more trees around the playground. When both sides of an argument are heard, people can come to a decision about how they should act on an issue.

Arguments are not always serious. Sometimes people present arguments to learn about and discuss opposing ideas.

Prove Your Point

When you make an argument, you are giving a set of **claims**, or statements, that prove why your position is right. To prove that your argument is correct, you need to give evidence that supports your claims. Without evidence, there is no way to prove that your claims are true. When you are evaluating an argument, it is up to you to decide whether the person making the argument has supported their claims with evidence.

*Bees are threatened by the use of harmful chemicals on plants. Without bees, many of the plants that humans rely on for food would not be **pollinated** and would die out.*

WHAT MAKES AN ARGUMENT?

Building an Argument

A good argument needs to be built carefully. A strong argument has the following features, or parts:

Core Argument

The **core argument** is the main point that you will try to prove in your argument. It is your position, or what you believe to be true. Arguments state the core argument in their introduction. An example of a core argument is:

> *Nuclear power is not a safe way to generate electricity.*

Claims

Your claims are the statements that support your core argument. An example of a claim is:

> *Nuclear power is not safe because accidents have the potential to be very dangerous for people and the environment.*

Reasons

Reasons are details that explain why you have made a claim. They are the statements that support your claim. An example of a reason is:

> *Nuclear power plants have had accidents that release **radioactive** material into the ground, oceans, and air around us. Radioactive material is extremely harmful to living things and can cause disease and death. Waste material from nuclear plants is also very difficult to dispose of and remains radioactive for thousands of years.*

The Chernobyl Exclusion Zone in Chernobyl, Ukraine, restricts access to the area that was contaminated after a nuclear explosion there in 1986. The abandoned town of Pripyat, near Chernobyl, once had a population of around 50,000.

Evidence

A good argument supports its reasons with evidence. Evidence could be **statistics** from a study of people affected by an issue, or facts about the topic. It could be a quotation from an interview with an expert on a topic. Without evidence, an argument cannot be proven to be true.

> Not everything you read is credible, so you need to assess if the evidence is valid. You can do this by asking questions such as:
> - Who is the author of the source of information? Are they qualified to speak on the subject?
> - Did the information come from a respected organization, such as a government website?
> - When was the source written? Information that is several years old may be out of date.
> - Do other sources have similar information? If not, you may need to evaluate whether the source is credible.

This is an example of credible evidence. It comes from two respected organizations.

> *The accident at the Chernobyl nuclear plant in Ukraine in 1986 was the worst nuclear accident in history. According to the World Nuclear Association, the U.S. Nuclear Regulatory Commission (NRC), and the UN Scientific Committee on the Effects of Atomic **Radiation** (UNSCEAR), within three months, 31 people died from radiation exposure and other effects of the accident.*

Counterclaims

To make an argument even stronger, a person needs to take note of the possible **counterclaims** against their argument. Counterclaims are the opposing claims to the argument. After making claims and giving reasons and evidence, a person making an argument should write down the strongest counterclaim against their argument. They should then respond to the counterclaim, using evidence, to prove why their argument is stronger. This is an example of a counterclaim:

> *Supporters of nuclear power point out that there have been very few accidents at nuclear power plants; accidents that do happen are the result of irregular circumstances. The Chernobyl reactor was poorly designed, and workers were not properly trained. The Fukushima plant opened in 1971. It was old when an earthquake caused an accident in 2011. According to UNSCEAR, it is unlikely that the Fukushima accident will cause future health problems for local people. However, given that it is impossible to remove the risk of human error or natural disasters, accidents remain a possibility.*

Conclusion

Your conclusion should restate your main argument and reasons. An example of a conclusion is:

> *Given the possibility of serious accidents at nuclear power plants, and the dangerous waste produced, it is clear that nuclear power is not safe.*

Evidence to support an argument can be found in many places, including in printed materials and online.

WHAT MAKES AN ARGUMENT?

Evaluating an Argument

You can evaluate an argument by looking at its features. Examine the argument below about wind energy and turbines. Does the argument include all of the features it needs to be a strong argument? When you have finished reading, decide if you think this argument is strong.

CORE ARGUMENT

Wind turbines should not be erected because of the danger they pose to animals and humans.

CLAIM

Wind turbines cause the deaths of flying animals.

REASON

Birds, bats, and other flying creatures are killed when they fly into wind turbines. Turbines are too much of a threat to local wildlife.

EVIDENCE

In the United States, the National Research Council estimated that in 2003, wind turbines killed between 20,000 and 37,000 birds. In the same year, the American Bird Conservancy stated that 10,000 to 40,000 birds are killed each year at U.S. wind farms.

Wind turbines threaten large birds such as the golden eagle. From 1997 to 2012, there were 85 eagle fatalities at 32 wind farms in the United States.

CLAIM

Wind farms cause **noise pollution** and health problems.

REASON

Some people living near wind turbines complain that they are very noisy and are causing them negative health effects, including headaches and sleep problems.

EVIDENCE

Sometimes wind turbines are built close to villages and towns. Even one wind turbine can be heard from hundreds of feet away. Local people have claimed to suffer from headaches, **tinnitus**, **vertigo**, and being unable to sleep properly. A 2011 study about wind turbine noise in New Zealand concluded that people living within 1.2 miles (1.9 km) of large wind farms said that they had, "lower overall quality of life, physical quality of life, and environmental quality of life. Those exposed to turbine noise also reported significantly lower sleep quality, and rated their environment as less restful."

COUNTERCLAIM

Proponents of wind power claim that, while it is true that wildlife deaths do occur as a result of wind turbines, the numbers are far lower than other causes of death for birds and other flying animals. A 2007 study by the National Research Council determined that, in a year, 976 million birds died after colliding with buildings, at least 130 million after hitting power lines, and 80 million from collisions with cars. Billions of power lines and buildings are already in place, so it is not practical to remove them to protect wildlife. Cars are also going to be on our roads for years to come. However, wind turbines are relatively new, and humans could easily stop building them or dismantle those already in place. Some of the animals affected by wind farms are endangered species. In the United States, wind turbines have killed endangered Indiana bats. Golden eagles have also been killed in northern California at the Altamont Pass Wind Resource Area.

CONCLUSION

The unnecessary deaths of birds and other flying creatures could be avoided if wind farms were not built. Noise pollution and health issues for local people could also be reduced. Wind farms also threaten the survival of the nation's endangered species. Therefore, they should not be built.

Some wind farms have hundreds of turbines that are used to generate electricity. The farms also use up a lot of land.

WHAT MAKES AN ARGUMENT?

Making a Great Argument

A core argument, claims, reasons, evidence, counterclaims, and the conclusion are the important parts of an argument. But there are also other elements that make a great argument.

Who Is Your Audience?

Arguments should be targeted toward their **audience**. People of different ages, **genders**, and backgrounds may have different viewpoints on an issue, and an argument should appeal to those views.

An audience made up of people who are interested in the topic must be approached differently from those who are not familiar with it. For example, a worker at a nuclear power plant may have stronger opinions about the safety of nuclear power than someone who is unfamiliar with nuclear power. People of different ages have different perspectives on issues. Younger people who use gadgets such as smartphones every day might have a different view on their effect on the environment than an older person who did not grow up with this technology. A person's lifestyle, their job, and where they live, may also affect how they feel about issues. When you make an argument, it is important to keep your audience in mind, and ensure that your claims and evidence will relate to them.

Introductions Count

Before stating your core argument, your introduction should get the reader interested in the topic. For example, an argument in favor of wind energy could state:

> *Did you know that wind power is not only a renewable source of energy, but it also creates jobs? In 2016, the U.S. wind industry employed more than 100,000 people. Wind Vision Report estimates that the industry could employ as many as 600,000 people by 2050.*

Arguments require convincing claims and strong evidence if they are to persuade people. How you present your argument is also important, and the words that you choose will add weight to an argument.

An employee of the wind power industry will have different opinions about its benefits and consequences than people who are not connected to the industry.

Clincher Conclusions

The conclusion is as important as your introduction. It restates your core argument and claims. Your conclusion should end with a **clincher**. This is a statement that strengthens your argument by capturing the reader's attention right at the end, so that he or she is more likely to think back on all the points you made.

In the argument about the benefits of wind energy, your clincher could state:

> *Given the advantages to the environment and the jobs that are created, wind energy is very beneficial. It is an important source of energy now and in the future.*

A clincher can also be a quote or a question that makes the reader think, such as:

> *Shouldn't we be using ways to generate energy that are not only renewable, but benefit the planet?*

Choose Your Words

The words you use and how you use them will help persuade people to see and appreciate your point of view. Words can appeal to someone's emotions and strengthen the evidence that you present. For example, referring to facts and statistics will back up your claims. Mentioning qualified experts and quoting from them will also make people more likely to believe you. Words can appeal to people's emotions by **emphasizing**, or stressing, things they care about. In the wind energy argument, words might emphasize the damage other energy sources, such as coal, caused to the environment as compared to wind power.

WHAT MAKES AN ARGUMENT?

Powerful Words

How effective an argument is often depends on the types of words used. **Rhetoric** is the art of using language effectively when writing or speaking. Rhetoric is used in persuasive speaking or writing by appealing to a reader or listener in different ways.

Persuasive Trio

There are three types of rhetoric: logos, pathos, and ethos.

Logos: Logos, which comes from the ancient Greek word for "logic," uses logic and reason to prove a point. Logos uses facts and statistics to support a point. A logical argument backed up with solid facts will help others consider your position, even if they do not agree with it. Here is an example of logos:

> *According to the World Health Organization (WHO), in 2006, there were up to 4,000 **thyroid cancer** cases in people who were children when they were exposed to radiation from the Chernobyl nuclear accident in 1986.*

Pathos: An argument based on pathos appeals to the audience's emotions. It often uses personal stories or facts that will make the audience feel a certain way. Stating the number of people who developed thyroid cancer is a good statistic, but it may not make the audience feel a certain way. However, a story about a person dealing with a health problem can make the audience care more about the issue. A personal story can also show why the statistic is important. Pathos should be used only to support your claim. It should not be used to confuse or frighten people in order to win an argument. A good example of pathos is:

> *Olga was only five years old when she was exposed to radiation from the Chernobyl nuclear accident. By the time she was 10, she showed the first signs of thyroid cancer, which is usually a very rare condition in children. Over the following years, Olga's thyroid gland became so enlarged that she had great difficulty breathing. Olga had very risky surgery to remove the growth and will now have to remain on medication for the rest of her life.*

Persuading other people to agree with you requires more than just facts and figures. You may also need to appeal to their emotions.

Ethos: Ethos is the way that a person can establish that he or she can be trusted. The tone and style of writing or speaking shows the person's qualifications and knowledge about an issue. Using reliable sources to build an argument can do this. The person can also tell the audience about his or her experience with the topic. Always respecting the opposing view and presenting it correctly to the audience can also establish trust. An example of ethos would be:

> *As an environmental columnist with* The New York Times, *I have toured hundreds of recycling facilities over the past 25 years. I believe that this particular plant is well-managed, fast, and safe.*

Plastic in the oceans kills fish, birds, and marine mammals. When animals are washed up onshore, there is often plastic waste in their stomachs.

LOOKING AT LANGUAGE

Read the following statement. Can you identify the rhetoric the author has used?

The amount of trash we produce by 2100 is expected to reach 11 million tons (10 million metric tons) per day. Trash is already being dumped on land and at sea, destroying ecosystems and causing the deaths of plants and animals. In 2015, it was estimated that there were 5.25 trillion pieces of plastic in the world's oceans. There were 269,000 tons (244,033 metric tons) floating on the surface, and even more in deeper parts of the oceans. How much damage do you think will have been done by the time your children are grown up? Don't you think that you should be making an effort today to protect the planet before it is too late?

Which types of rhetoric does the statement use to appeal to the audience? What words or phrases make you think so?

WHAT MAKES AN ARGUMENT?

Where Do You Stand?

Use what you know about the features of arguments and what makes arguments strong to evaluate the two arguments about recycling below. Which argument do you feel is stronger? Why?

Recycling Is Protecting the Environment.

Recycling protects the environment because it helps us preserve, or use less of, the planet's resources. When we recycle products, the materials in them can be reused to create new products. This means that we don't have to extract new oil, coal, or metal **ore** from the earth to make them. For example, aluminum is easy to recycle and can be reused again and again. Making aluminum cans from recycled metal saves not only aluminum, but also 92 percent of the cost of producing a can from new metal. Recycling a single aluminum can saves enough energy to run a television for three hours.

Recycling paper saves energy and prevents trees from being cut down. Making new paper from recycled paper uses just 60 percent of the energy that is needed to make new paper from trees. The production of recycled paper also creates 44 percent fewer **greenhouse gases**, 53 percent less wastewater, and 39 percent less waste. According to the Environmental Protection Agency (EPA), recycling glass rather than creating it from new materials creates 50 percent less water pollution. Around 80 percent of glass containers are also simply washed and reused.

Some people say recycling is not a complete solution to waste problems, as it is expensive and not all materials can be recycled. It is true that there are still around 2,500 active landfills in the United States, which are polluting the land, water, and air. However, recycling is leading to a reduction in new landfills. For example, in 2016, San Francisco and Oakland, California said they would stop sending garbage to landfills within four years. In Ontario, Canada, 147 landfills have closed since 1999.

Since recycling helps to conserve the planet's natural resources by reusing materials and saving energy, recycling is protecting the environment. Recycling is also reducing the need for new landfills. Without a doubt, recycling is protecting the environment.

Clothing can be recycled, too. The materials are not usually made into new clothes but used in other products, such as carpet padding.

Recycling Is Not Protecting the Environment.

Recycling is not protecting the environment because it uses up a lot of energy and too much waste still ends up in landfills. The recycling process uses up energy and creates waste products. Recycled materials need to be sorted and separated at a recycling plant using machines such as conveyor belts and robotic arms, which use a lot of energy. Recycling plants and the trucks that collect recyclable materials also usually run on fossil fuels. The greenhouse gases that these produce then pollute the environment. Energy is also needed to melt down and reshape recyclable materials, such as glass and metal.

Recycling is not effective, which means that many products end up in landfills anyway. Many types of plastic cannot be recycled and end up in landfills. Polyvinyl chloride (PVC or vinyl), polystyrene, and bisphenol A are almost never recycled because they cannot be melted and reformed. PVC is found in plastic wraps, food and detergent containers, and vinyl pipes and flooring. Polystyrene is used in Styrofoam cups, takeout containers, egg cartons, and disposable cutlery. Bisphenol A is found in some plastic baby bottles, water jugs, lids, and sunglasses.

Proponents of recycling say the process does use energy, but for many items, this is less than when products are produced from raw materials. For example, according to the Environmental Paper Network's Paper Calculator, it takes 31 percent less energy to produce recycled paper than new paper. However, the recycling process still does not work well. Fewer than one percent of plastic bags are currently recycled, which means that in the United States, around 300,000 tons (272,155 metric tons) of plastic bags are dumped in landfills every year. Americans drink around 778 million cans of soda per day, but only around 144 million cans are recycled.

Recycling is not yet doing enough to protect the environment. More could be done to reduce the energy use of the recycling process, including using electric vehicles for pickups. More effective recycling techniques need to be developed for all materials before we can say that recycling is truly protecting the environment.

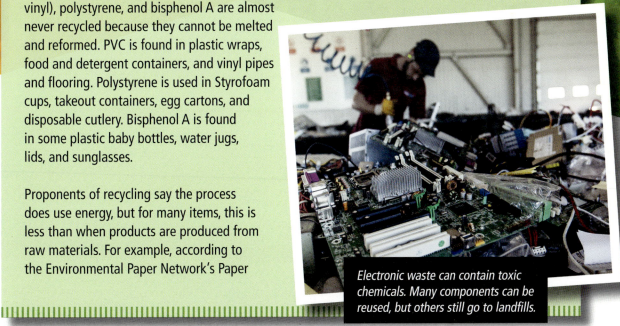

Electronic waste can contain toxic chemicals. Many components can be reused, but others still go to landfills.

CHAPTER 3
SHOULD CLEAR-CUTTING FORESTS FOR AGRICULTURE BE ALLOWED?

Clear-cutting is when all of the trees in an area of forest are cut down. Clear-cutting is sometimes done during **logging**, when trees are sold as timber for construction or **pulp** for papermaking. Clear-cutting is also done to create open land for **agriculture**, or farming.

Trees in forests are cut down for many reasons. Cutting down trees is not always harmful to the forest. Selective logging is a practice in which only certain trees are cut down. Clear-cutting can even be used for good, when foresters clear-cut, then replant, a section of forest to encourage the growth of new tree species and forest ecosystems. But widespread clear-cutting concerns many people who feel that cutting down huge areas of trees damages the ecosystems there beyond repair.

In South America, Africa, and Southeast Asia, large areas of tropical forest are cleared for planting crops, and for cattle ranching, which requires a lot of land. In Africa, around 15,000 square miles (38,850 sq km) of forest are lost every year. In the last 50 years, around 17 percent of the Amazon rain forest has been lost.

Although we most often hear about the clear-cutting of tropical rain forests such as the Amazon, the practice is also used in North America and Europe. The northern **coniferous** forests of Scandinavia, Russia, and North America are also under threat from clear-cutting. In some parts of the world, including the United States and Canada, governments regulate, or place limits on, clear-cutting. For example, laws in Canada limit the size of an area that will be clear-cut. Laws in the United States and Canada say that clear-cut forests need to be replanted.

However, most clear-cutting takes place in the **developing world**, particularly in countries such as Brazil in South America, the Democratic Republic of Congo in Africa, and Indonesia in Asia. In these countries, there are not always government policies that regulate clear-cutting. In these places, clear-cutting for agriculture is common.

Soybeans are a very important crop in South America. Creating fields for the crops means that large areas of the Amazon are cut down every year.

Once trees are cut down or burned to clear an area of tropical forest, cattle are able to graze there.

Benefits and Dangers

When farmers clear-cut an area of forest, the new, open area receives more sunlight and rain, so that crops can be planted, or grass can grow for grazing. Supporters of clear-cutting believe that the practice brings great benefits to the local community, particularly in developing countries. It allows large farms to be created that provide profitable jobs for the people there.

However, the animal species that used to live in an area of clear-cut forest may become at risk from loss of habitat. In addition, without trees to hold the soil in place, **soil erosion** can take place. This means that the soil is slowly washed away by rain and streams, so that, eventually, very little can grow in the area. Farming also uses chemicals, such as **pesticides**, **herbicides**, and fertilizers. These help farmers grow crops, but can damage local wildlife and trickle into streams, causing a greater impact.

So, what are the arguments for and against clear-cutting forests for agriculture?

FOREST FACTS

Here are some statistics about forests and their importance:

- Forests cover 30 percent of the planet's land.
- 70 percent of Earth's plants and animals live in forests.
- 20 percent of the world's **oxygen** is produced by the Amazon rain forest.
- Every minute, an area of forest the size of 20 football fields is cut down somewhere on Earth.

Clear-Cutting Forests for Agriculture Should Be Allowed.

Clear-cutting creates potential for agriculture and jobs for those who need it, so it should not be disallowed. Clear-cutting is a good method of creating more farmland. Many tropical crops, such as citrus fruits, bananas, coffee, tea, soybeans, rice, and rubber, need a lot of space to grow. To make money, crops need to be grown on a large scale on big **plantations**, where the water use and workforce can be best managed. Clear-cutting is the best, and often the only, method of creating a large area of farmland or land for grazing cattle. The practice allows a farm to begin operations swiftly and provide benefits to the local **economy** quickly. Every year, 50,000 square miles (129,500 sq km) of forest in developing countries in South America, Africa, and Southeast Asia are turned into farmland. For example, in Indonesia, 120,000 square miles (310,799 sq km) of land are used for farming, which is around one-third of the total land available. Currently, around 49 million Indonesians, more than 40 percent of the nation's workforce, are employed in agriculture. So it is clear that more land is needed for farming, not less.

Clear-cutting improves people's lives in developing countries. If more farmland is created there, people can make more money by selling farmed goods. Local people are also able to get jobs on the new ranches and farms. The trees removed from an area during clear-cutting are sold as timber, which also brings money to local people. When an area becomes more prosperous, or makes more money, schools, hospitals, and other facilities are likely to improve, leading to a better quality of life for the entire community.

*About 30 percent of Indonesian land is used for farming. There are large plantations growing crops for **export**, as well as farms serving local people.*

Many familiar foods, such as bananas and other fruits, are grown on farms in the developing world. They are then exported to other countries.

Around the world, 1.6 billion people rely on forest products, including timber and crops grown on clear-cut land, for their livelihood. More than 25 million people live in the Brazilian Amazon, the majority of them working on farmland. Local farmers in the Mato Grosso region say that the financial benefits of clear-cutting outweigh the risks of breaking the laws intended to prevent deforestation. "This is a good time for us in agriculture, especially in soy, especially in Mato Grosso. This is now the global center for soy," says Silvésio de Oliveira, director of the state's Soy and Maize Association. Oliveira is asking the Brazilian government to reduce the proportion of protected forest on farmers' land so they can plant more crops.

Some people argue that clear-cutting damages the environment, can push wildlife to extinction, and causes soil erosion. Clearing areas for large farms also means that fertilizers and pesticides will be used, further damaging the local soil and water quality. Although clear-cutting does cause some damage to the environment, these issues are outweighed by the financial benefits to local people. The fact that they live in a forested area should not prevent them from earning a living. According to the World Bank, more than 1.3 billion people live in extreme poverty, on less than $1.25 a day. One billion children worldwide are living in poverty. Creating new farming jobs by clearing forests for farmland could help reduce the number of people living in poverty.

Due to the benefits to the local community, clear-cutting should be allowed. Do we really have the right to prevent people in the developing world from improving their daily lives and their futures, too?

Clear-Cutting Forests for Agriculture Should Not Be Allowed.

The harm that clear-cutting causes to ecosystems outweighs its farming benefits, so it should not be allowed. Clear-cutting destroys the habitats of plants and animals. Within an ecosystem, all the living things work together and depend on each other—including trees. Even small-scale clear-cutting disrupts this system. Some animal species could become extinct as a result of clear-cutting. Habitat loss happens when an ecosystem is changed by human activity, such as farming, mining, building, or diverting rivers and streams. An area can no longer support the wildlife, which needs food, water, shelter, and places to raise their offspring. Animals and plants all depend on each other. If the place where they all live is damaged, the ecosystem breaks down. Forests cover one-third of the planet's land area. Many of the world's most threatened species live in forests. We are losing the equivalent of 27 soccer fields of forest every minute. According to the World Wildlife Fund (WWF), species threatened with extinction by deforestation include the Bornean and Sumatran orangutans, Sumatran elephant, Sumatran tiger, white-cheeked spider monkey, giant otter, bare-faced tamarin, and many more. Professor Robert Ewers of Imperial College London, United Kingdom, predicts that if deforestation in the Amazon continues at the current rate, at least 15 mammal, 30 bird, and 10 amphibian species are expected to die out locally by 2050.

Orangutans are an endangered species. It is estimated that there are around 104,700 in Borneo and approximately 7,500 in Sumatra.

Madagascar loses so much soil to erosion that many of the island's rivers are red in color.

Clear-cutting causes soil erosion, damages water quality, and leads to more fertilizers, herbicides, and pesticides being used. Soil erosion often occurs after clear-cutting for agricultural land. This means that the soil is washed away, making the growing of crops and plants increasingly difficult. Soil erosion can also lower the quality of the area's water, as soil and rocks wash into nearby rivers, streams, lakes, and **reservoirs**. This will affect the health of locally grown crops as well as plants and animals that depend on the water. Erosion has been a major factor in the loss of around one-third of the world's **fertile** land since 1960. Around 38,610 square miles (100,000 sq km) of **arable** land are still lost around the world every year. Every year, around 860 million tons (780 million metric tons) of **topsoil** are lost in Costa Rica.

Large plantations that produce crops often use a lot of fertilizer and herbicide to make sure that the plants are healthy. These chemicals often wash into rivers and streams, damage the environment, and cause illnesses for local people. More than 95 percent of herbicides and 98 percent of insecticides reach species other than those they are targeting. Around 30 percent of the world's amphibian species are now endangered because of habitat loss, disease, and exposure to pesticides and fertilizers, according to Tiffany Garcia, associate professor of wildlife science at Ohio State University's College of Agricultural Sciences.

Some people believe that clear-cutting for agriculture should be allowed because it helps the local economy. In 2009, research published by Imperial College London showed that the benefit to the local economy is short-lived. The soil quality rapidly worsens, which means that farming and cattle ranching can only last a few years before the land cannot support it. In the meantime, large numbers of people have moved into the local area hoping to find work. When the soil erodes, the area has less usable land, more people, and lower income than before.

The clear-cutting of forests for agriculture should not be allowed because it destroys the habitats of endangered species. Clear-cutting also results in soil erosion and pollution, which make the land unusable. Any benefit to locals is short-lived, but the environmental damage is long-term.

SHOULD CLEAR-CUTTING FORESTS FOR AGRICULTURE BE ALLOWED?

STATE YOUR CASE

When it comes to any issue, you have to look at arguments on both sides before you decide where you stand. Remember the features of effective arguments when you consider the arguments for and against clear-cutting forests for agriculture. Which side's argument do you think is stronger? Why do you think so? Give reasons for your answers. Use the "In Summary: For and Against" list to help you figure out your decision, and state your own case.

IN SUMMARY: FOR AND AGAINST

For Clear-Cutting Forests for Agriculture

Clear-cutting in the developing world is a good method of creating more farmland.

- Many tropical crops, such as citrus fruits, bananas, coffee, tea, soybeans, rice, oil palms, cacao, and rubber, need a lot of space to grow.
- For such crops to be profitable, they need to be grown on big plantations, where water use and workers can be best managed.
- In tropical areas, clear-cutting is often the only method of creating a large area of farmland or land for grazing cattle.

Clear-cutting helps provide jobs and income for people who need it.

- Creating more farmland means that there will be more farming jobs for local people, and more money can be made from selling farmed goods.
- The felled trees can be sold as timber.
- When an area becomes more prosperous, local facilities, such as schools and hospitals, improve, leading to a better quality of life.
- Around the world, 1.6 billion people rely on forest products for their livelihood, including timber and crops grown on clear-cut land.

Beans from the cacao tree are used to make chocolate. The trees first grew in tropical regions in the Americas, but most are now grown in West Africa.

Against Clear-Cutting Forests for Agriculture

Clear-cutting destroys the habitats of plants and animals.

- Clear-cutting creates habitat loss and disrupts the balance of ecosystems.
- According to WWF, species threatened with extinction by deforestation include the Bornean and Sumatran orangutans, Sumatran elephant, Sumatran tiger, white-cheeked spider monkey, giant otter, bare-faced tamarin, and many more.
- If deforestation in the Amazon continues at the current rate, at least 15 mammal, 30 bird, and 10 amphibian species are expected to die out locally by 2050.

Clear-cutting causes soil erosion, damages water quality, and leads to more fertilizers, herbicides, and pesticides being used.

- Soil erosion often occurs after clear-cutting for agricultural land. This means that farms cannot support crops or animals long-term, leaving the area with less usable land, more people, and lower income than before.
- Soil erosion can also lower the quality of the area's water, as soil and rocks wash into nearby rivers, streams, lakes, and reservoirs.
- Large plantations use a lot of fertilizer and herbicides, which can damage the environment, be washed into rivers and streams, and cause illnesses for local people.

The red-backed poison frog is found in tropical rain forest in South America. Its habitat is under intense threat from clear-cutting.

CHAPTER 4
DOES BOTTLED WATER DO MORE HARM THAN GOOD?

Humans need water to survive, because our bodies need to keep **hydrated**. Water is better for our health than other drinks, as it contains no calories or sugar. Bottled water is a popular drink choice for many people. It is convenient and often considered to be a cleaner water source than water from taps. In some areas where water from taps is not safe to drink, bottled water is relied on. However, bottled water comes in plastic bottles, which cause a major environmental problem.

Bottled or Tap

Bottled water is very convenient to carry when traveling, or when at school or on an outing. Americans consume about 12.8 billion gallons (48 billion liters) of bottled water per year, about 40 gallons (151 liters) per person. Canadians drink about 0.6 billion gallons (2.3 billion liters) of bottled water per year, about 18 gallons (68 liters) per person. However, bottled water can be expensive compared to the water that comes from our taps at home. Tap water is safe to drink in most areas in developed countries. Governments usually have safety rules that say how tap water should be **treated** to make it safe for drinking. Water used for bottling must also be from an approved source. Bottled water can be natural spring water, or tap water that has had extra treatment.

However, the quality of tap water is not the same in every area. Harmful substances, such as pesticides used in farming, that might be washed into rivers and streams can occasionally contaminate tap water. If tap water has to travel through lead pipes, which were used in the past, the lead can seep into the water and cause health issues, such as developmental problems in children. Lead pipes are not common in North America. In some areas, even in developed countries, tap water is not safe to drink. For example, some First Nations communities

People should drink six to eight glasses of water every day to keep healthy, although some are fine with more or less than this.

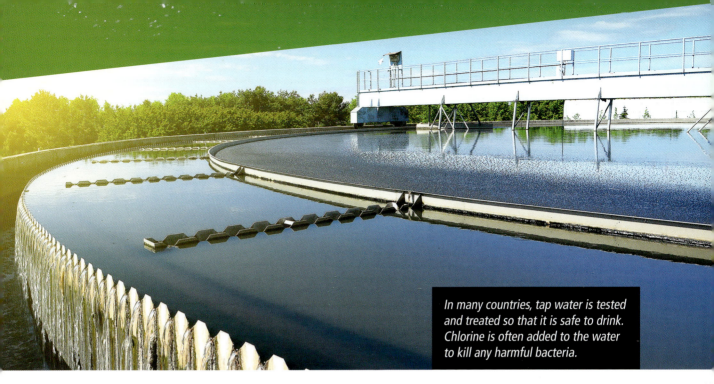

In many countries, tap water is tested and treated so that it is safe to drink. Chlorine is often added to the water to kill any harmful bacteria.

in Canada do not have the option of drinking water from the tap unless it is boiled, and may choose to use bottled water. Some communities have been without safe tap water for decades.

Questions About Bottled Water

Some people believe that there is no difference between bottled water and tap water. They argue that bottled water is just one way that huge companies make money. A main concern about bottled water is the plastic bottles. Millions of plastic bottles are thrown into the garbage or into landfills and not recycled. Although bottled water might be good for us, it may not be good for the environment.

So, what are the arguments for and against bottled water?

BOTTLED WATER BY NUMBERS

Here are some interesting statistics about bottled water:

- In 2017, the worldwide bottled water industry was worth more than $198.5 billion.
- In 2016, 12.8 billion gallons (48 billion liters) of bottled water were sold in the United States.
- Three out of 10 Canadian households drink bottled water.
- Of the 50 billion plastic water bottles used each year in the United States, only around 12 billion are recycled.

Bottled Water Does More Good Than Harm.

Bottled water is a good drinking option because it is healthy, it is convenient, and it is vital in situations where safe tap water is not available. Bottled water is clean and healthy. The water is purified before it is bottled and is inspected by the government to prove that it is safe to drink. To be healthy, our bodies need to keep hydrated. We can carry bottled water wherever we go, which is a great advantage in hot weather when it is particularly important to drink plenty of water. Bottled water is convenient and readily available in grocery stores, vending machines, restaurants, and school cafeterias. It is easy to carry and is a convenient and healthy way to stay hydrated throughout the day. In 2015, 86 percent of U.S. consumers bought bottled water. A 2017 survey by the International Bottled Water Association (IBWA) learned that 82 percent of people drank bottled water because it is readily available, and that 74 percent said that resealable bottles are important to them. "Americans are looking for a healthful way to quench their thirst, and bottled water is convenient, and compared to high-sugar, high-calorie choices, it's a good choice," says Stephen Kay, vice president of the IBWA. Many people prefer the taste of bottled water. The IBWA also states that around 70 percent of people that buy bottled water do so because they prefer the taste to that of tap water.

Bottled water is also essential in situations where clean drinking water is not available from a tap. After natural disasters, such as hurricanes or tsunamis, tap water is often contaminated and is unsafe to drink. Bottled water is a useful and lifesaving solution as it allows for safe water to be distributed to people who need it. For example, in 2005, Hurricane Katrina left millions of people

Athletes in particular need to drink enough water. People who run long races need to keep hydrated throughout the event.

The National Guard handed out bottled water in Flint, Michigan, in 2016. The local tap water had been contaminated by lead and other harmful substances.

in Louisiana and Mississippi without drinkable tap water, so bottled water had to be supplied by the National Guard. In some communities, tap water is not safe to drink at any time of year. It is important for these communities to have the option to drink bottled water, as they can be sure it is safe. According to the Council of Canadians, in 2018, more than 80 First Nations communities had unsafe tap water, forcing them to boil tap water before drinking or to buy bottled water.

Critics of bottled water argue that it may not be completely safe. In the United States, the Food & Drug Administration (FDA) does not require water manufacturers to disclose where the bottled water came from, how it is treated, or report any contamination. However, although not required by the FDA, many bottled water companies provide details of the source of the water. They also provide contact details on labels, so that people can call the company to ask about the source or safety procedures if they have any concerns. Bottled water companies' production must follow the FDA's current good manufacturing practice (CGMP) regulations. These state that bottled water must be sampled, analyzed, and **sanitary**, or hygienic. The FDA inspects bottled water plants, and some U.S. states require that bottled water companies are licensed once a year.

Based on the evidence, bottled water is clean, healthy, and convenient. It is also essential in situations when clean tap water is not an option. There is no need to stop buying bottled water to quench your thirst, as bottled water undoubtedly does more good than harm.

Bottled Water Does More Harm Than Good.

Bottled water is harmful to our health, our wallets, and the environment. Bottled water is not always safe. **Contaminants** and other harmful substances have been found in bottled water. In 2018, the WHO announced a health review after more than 90 percent of the most popular brands of bottled water were found to contain tiny pieces of plastic. Analysis of 259 bottles of 11 different brands from 19 locations in nine countries found an average of 325 plastic particles for every 34 ounces (1 liter) of bottled water. In 2015, Niagara Bottling in the United States recalled its bottled water from stores after finding it was contaminated with the harmful bacterium *E. coli*. In 2017, U.S. supermarket chain Kroger found mold that can cause serious health problems in its Comforts for Baby brand of purified water. "Bottled water generally is no cleaner, or safer, or healthier than tap water," according to a report by Food and Water Watch. "In fact, the federal government requires far more rigorous and frequent safety testing and monitoring of **municipal** drinking water." The cost of purifying, bottling, and transporting the water is added to the price. Around 90 percent of the price of bottled water is for the packaging. According to *Consumer Reports* in 2011, a 16.9-ounce (500 ml) bottle filled with tap water costs about 0.13 cents. Filling this with tap water every day for a year would cost 48 cents. Spending $1 on the same sized bottle of water would cost $365 per year, which is quite a price difference.

Plastic bottles damage the environment. Bottled water is placed in plastic containers made from fossil fuels, such as oil, which are not sustainable resources. Many plastic bottles end up in landfills and in the ocean, where they are a threat to wildlife. Around 50 million plastic water bottles are used in the United States in a year. This plastic

According to Business Insider, *bottled water costs 300 times more than tap water.*

Millions of plastic bottles are recycled around the world every year. However, even more end up in landfills, oceans, and other ecosystems. More work needs to be done to ensure that more bottles are recycled.

is made from 17 million barrels of oil. However, only around 20 percent of plastic bottles are recycled. In 2008, more than 2,480,000 tons (2,250,000 metric tons) of plastic bottles and containers were thrown away rather than being recycled. Every year, more than 8 million tons (7.2 million metric tons) of plastic, much of it plastic bottles, is dumped into the oceans. By 2050, it is estimated there will be more plastic in the oceans by weight than there are fish, according to research by the Ellen MacArthur Foundation.

Supporters of bottled water say that people are always going to want to buy beverages when they are away from home, at school, work, the movie theater, or the gym. A bottle of water is the healthiest option, as it contains no sugar or calories. The average can of soda contains around 10 teaspoons of sugar. Consuming too much sugar is bad for our teeth and likely to make us gain weight. Although bottled water may not be bad for our health, it is bad for the environment. Every year, the bottled water industry uses 1.5 million tons (1.4 million metric tons) of plastic to package water. Making plastic and disposing of it releases toxic chemicals into the environment. One plastic water bottle will not even start to decompose for 700 years.

Bottled water does more harm than good because it is expensive and may not always be safe to drink. The plastic bottles are not always recycled and end up either in landfills or in the ocean, doing major damage to the environment.

STATE YOUR CASE

When it comes to any issue, you have to look at arguments on both sides before you decide where you stand. Remember the features of effective arguments when you consider the arguments for and against bottled water. Which argument do you think is the strongest? Give reasons for your answers. Use the "In Summary: For and Against" list to help you figure out your decision, and state your own case.

IN SUMMARY: FOR AND AGAINST

For Bottled Water

Bottled water is clean and healthy.

- Quality standard regulations at the FDA determine the maximum levels of contaminants allowed in bottled water.
- The FDA inspects bottled water plants, and some states require that companies are licensed once a year.
- Bottled water is healthier than sugary sodas.
- Bottled water is essential when safe tap water is not available. After natural disasters, tap water may become contaminated or unavailable. Often, bottled water is distributed to people who need it.
- There are hundreds of communities in the United States and Canada that do not have safe drinking water and may need to drink bottled water instead.
- Around 70 percent of people who buy bottled water do so because they prefer the taste to that of tap water.

Bottled water is convenient and readily available.

- Bottled water is available in stores, vending machines, restaurants, and school cafeterias.
- Water in resealable bottles is easy to carry, which makes it useful on the go.

Bottled water is a great option when traveling, especially on long journeys where there are limited places to stop to buy drinks.

Against Bottled Water

Bottled water is not always safe and is also very expensive.

- Contaminants and other harmful substances have been found in bottled water.
- In 2018, WHO announced a health review after more than 90 percent of the most popular brands of bottled water were found to contain tiny pieces of plastic.
- In the United States, the federal government requires more rigorous and frequent testing of municipal water than bottled water.
- Bottled water is expensive because of the cost of bottling and transportation.

Plastic bottles damage the environment.

- Around 50 million plastic water bottles are used in the United States every year.
- This plastic is made from 17 million barrels of oil, which is not a renewable resource.
- Only around 20 percent of plastic bottles are recycled.
- Every year, more than 8 million tons (7.2 million metric tons) of plastic, much of it plastic bottles, is dumped into the oceans.

Bottles that are not recycled often end up in the ocean or washed up on beaches all over the world.

CHAPTER 5
SHOULD SCHOOLS GO PAPERLESS?

Although much of the paper used in North America is recycled, paper use still contributes to deforestation. More and more business and learning is now being carried out on computer screens. Should we completely cut out paper use by going paperless? Schools are one place where a lot of paper could be saved.

Problems with Paper

In 2017, 65.8 percent of paper in the United States was recycled. Most paper used in North America comes from managed forests, where the cutting down of trees is balanced against the planting of new trees. However, paper use still contributes to deforestation all over the planet. In 2014, 93 percent of paper still came from newly cut trees, and 14 percent of all the wood harvested around the world was used to make paper.

The process of logging trees and making paper also uses up a lot of energy. Worldwide, the pulp and paper industry is the fifth-largest energy consumer, accounting for around 4 percent of worldwide energy use. Paper production also uses a lot of water to turn wood into a mush that can be pressed into sheets, then dried. It takes 2.6 gallons (10 liters) of water to produce one 8.5 x 11 inch (U.S. letter size) sheet of paper.

Schools use a great deal of paper for books, art, notebooks, tests, quizzes, and reports. There are around 960,000 schools in the United States. A typical school uses around 2,000 sheets of paper a day, or around 360,000 sheets per school year. This adds up to 345 billion sheets across the country. Around 40 percent of the waste produced by schools in the United States is made up of paper. Even if all this paper is recycled, energy and time is wasted in transporting, sorting, recycling, packaging, and redistributing this paper.

However, computers and the Internet have greatly changed education in recent decades. Teachers can do presentations on computers and laptops, deliver courses and quizzes electronically, and give students their school reports and grades by email. Students are also able to research facts online,

In the United States, around two-thirds of used paper is recycled. In Canada, only around a quarter of paper is recycled.

so perhaps even school libraries are unnecessary today. Many schools are working toward going completely paperless in the future.

Too Much Technology?

However, some people believe that going paperless will force us to be too dependent on computer technology. While it is important to reduce the use of paper, they feel that going completely paperless may not be the best option. If paper was not used in classrooms, schools would need to spend extra money on technology instead. Laptops and tablets are more expensive than paper. Digital learning tools, such as apps or online library subscriptions, also come at a price. Many educators worry that some important skills, such as handwriting, drawing, and painting, would be lost if schools were completely paperless.

So, what are the arguments for and against schools going paperless?

People have been using paper at school for a long time. Some people argue that computers cannot completely replace paper because some skills are learned using paper only.

Schools Should Go Paperless.

Going paperless would help schools save money because they would no longer have to buy books and paper for classrooms every year. This money can be used to buy electronic equipment or other things the school needs. Digital information is also more efficient for school office workers. It is easy to access and does not require storage space such as filing cabinets. Digital information is also less likely to be lost or damaged in fires or floods. Each year, an average school spends around $25,000 on paper. It also spends money on paper-related expenses such as ink for printers and copiers. For example, the cost of black ink cartridges bought three times a year is between $60 and $120. If a school has a number of printers, this cost adds up. Going paperless would not involve an immense cost, since in the United States, 84 percent of schools already have high-speed Internet, and 98 percent of U.S. schools already have more than one computer in the classroom. **E-books** are cheaper than printed books. Some printed books can cost between $10 and $20, whereas some e-books are priced at just $0.99 or are free online. If e-books replaced printed books, it would also free up space in areas formerly used for libraries that might be used for science labs, physical education, or drama.

Paperless schools would be better for the environment. Fewer trees will be cut down to make paper, there will be less pollution from paper mills, less wasted paper in landfills, and less garbage created by waste from things such as printers, copiers, and ink cartridges. More than 68 million trees are cut down every year in the United States to make paper. One tree can produce around 500 sheets of paper. Making that amount of paper from a tree releases around 110 pounds (50 kg) of carbon dioxide into the atmosphere during the production process at a mill. According to the EPA, more than 100 million **toner** cartridges and more than 400 million ink

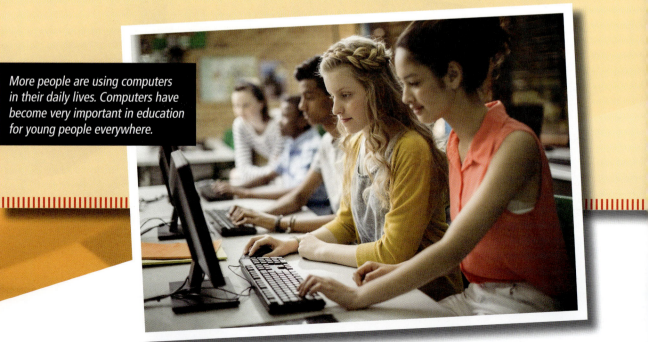

More people are using computers in their daily lives. Computers have become very important in education for young people everywhere.

The pulp and paper industry uses around 40 percent of all the wood that is traded around the world for products such as paper, tissues, and cardboard.

cartridges are sent to landfills every year in the United States. According to the EPA, 31 percent of the solid waste in the United States in 2008 was paper. As it breaks down in a landfill, paper produces methane gas that harms the environment.

Some people argue that, if schools become paperless, some students would suffer if they do not work well with technology and prefer to express themselves on paper. Some students might also lose skills such as handwriting and drawing if schools went paperless. This would affect their education and could lead to them falling behind their peers at school. However, students need to work with technology to be prepared for the workforce after school. An increasing number of jobs rely on computer skills. For example, according to the United States Department of Labor Statistics, more than 50 percent of current jobs require technology skills, and this figure will rise to 77 percent in the next 10 years.

Schools should go paperless: It would make them more efficient and save money. Going paperless would also save trees, reduce garbage in landfills, and reduce pollution in the atmosphere. Working onscreen or online would have many benefits for students today and tomorrow.

Schools Should Not Go Paperless.

Going paperless will influence students to be too dependent on technology, cause health problems, and harm skill development. If students use computers exclusively to learn at school, they will become too dependent on technology at an early age. College students are already very dependent on technology. A recent study of 500 college students learned that 73 percent believed that they could not study without using technology. Technology already affects the ability of young people to interact with each other. "As children and parents are attaching more and more to technology, they're detaching from each other, and we know as a species we need to connect," says **pediatric occupational therapist** Cris Rowan. Being too dependent on technology also means that work can be lost in the event that a computer breaks down. Lessons might halt entirely if Internet access were lost. Parents will also be required to provide technology at home for students to complete homework. Not every parent can afford this. Eyecare professionals such as Vancouver optometrist Mini Randhawa are warning that lengthy hours in front of a screen is causing an "**epidemic**" among children of nearsightedness, so they cannot see very far.

The human brain works better when using a pen and paper. Humans engage in problem-solving and **critical thinking** better when they are able to jot down ideas with paper and pen. Many students are also better able to express their creativity with paper. This is especially true with art, but also with storytelling and essay-writing. With kindergarten and lower-grade children, learning needs to be simple. Some young children

Young people have grown up using technology. Many are overly dependent on their phones, laptops, and tablets.

Paper still has a role to play at school. Children and adults can benefit from creating on paper.

might experience difficulties with learning computer skills at the same time as basic reading, writing, and math. A 2016 study by Pam Mueller of Princeton University, New Jersey, and Dan Oppenheimer of the University of California, Los Angeles, determined that taking notes by hand about what a teacher says helps students to understand and remember what they are learning, but typing notes means students do not give much thought to what they are actually hearing. In 2016, researchers from the Massachusetts Institute of Technology (MIT) found that students who were not allowed to use digital devices or laptops in class performed better on exams than those allowed to use computers and go online.

Some people believe students should use computers at school and for homework, since schools should be preparing students for the workplace, where there is a computer on every desk. However, while many jobs in the future will depend on technology, people will still need skills for other jobs, such as those requiring creativity. In the coming decades, musicians, artists, and chefs will still be needed, as will people working in jobs where they attend to the needs of others, such as in nursing or social work. Evidence shows that using paper during learning supports the problem-solving and critical thinking skills needed for these jobs.

Schools should not go paperless because students are already too dependent on technology, which is affecting their health, learning, and development of social skills. If schools go paperless, it will also be unfair to students who prefer to work with paper and may be more suited to careers that involve creativity or caring for others.

STATE YOUR CASE

When it comes to any issue, you have to look at arguments on both sides before you decide where you stand. Remember the features of effective arguments when you consider the arguments for and against schools going paperless. Which argument do you think is the most convincing? Why do you think that one is better than the other? Give reasons for your answers. Use the "In Summary: For and Against" list to help you figure out your decision, and state your own case.

IN SUMMARY: FOR AND AGAINST

For Schools Going Paperless

Paperless schools would be more efficient.

- Schools will save money if they no longer have to buy books and paper.
- Digital information is more efficient for school office workers.
- Going paperless would not be too expensive since, in the United States, 84 percent of schools already have high-speed Internet, and 98 percent already have more than one computer in the classroom.
- E-books are cheaper than printed books, saving library costs.

Paperless schools would be better for the environment.

- More than 68 million trees are cut down every year in the United States to make paper.
- Making paper from one tree releases around 110 pounds (50 kg) of carbon dioxide.
- More than 100 million toner cartridges and 400 million ink cartridges are sent to landfills every year in the United States.
- In 2008, 31 percent of the solid waste in the United States was paper.
- As it breaks down in a landfill, paper produces methane gas that harms the environment.

Paper mills used to create a lot of pollution. They have become cleaner in more recent years, but still cause damage to the environment.

Against Schools Going Paperless

Students are already too dependent on technology.

- Children and teenagers already have too much screen time.
- Technology already affects the ability of young people to interact with each other.
- Too much screen time can damage eyesight.
- Computers can crash or break down, losing people's work.
- If parents were expected to supply laptops and tablets for homework, this would exclude children in lower-income families.

The human brain works better when using a pen and paper.

- Humans engage in problem-solving and critical thinking better when they are able to jot down ideas with paper and pen.
- Many students are also better able to express their creativity on paper.
- With kindergarten and lower-grade children, learning needs to be simple. Learning computer skills may complicate basic education for young students.
- In 2016, researchers from the Massachusetts Institute of Technology found that computers have a negative effect on academic performance.

Although e-books have become popular, some people will always love to hold and read a book made from paper.

BIBLIOGRAPHY

The Environment Today and Tomorrow

"About Renewable Energy." Natural Resources Canada, 2017. www.nrcan.gc.ca/energy/renewable-electricity/7295

"Biomass Explained: Waste-to-Energy (Municipal Solid Waste)." U.S. Energy Information Administration. www.eia.gov/energyexplained/?page=biomass_waste_to_energy

"Canada at a Glance: Environment Edition." Statistics Canada. www150.statcan.gc.ca/n1/pub/12-581-x/12-581-x2017001-eng.htm

What Makes an Argument?

"Advantages and Challenges of Wind Energy." Office of Energy Efficiency & Renewable Energy. www.energy.gov/eere/wind/advantages-and-challenges-wind-energy

Bryce, Robert. "Wind Energy, Noise Pollution." *National Review*, February 2, 2012. www.nationalreview.com/2012/02/wind-energy-noise-pollution-robert-bryce

Casey, Zoe. "Wind Farms: A Noisy Neighbor?" *Renewable Energy World*, February 21, 2013. www.renewableenergyworld.com/articles/2013/02/wind-farms-a-noisy-neighbor.html

"Chernobyl Accident 1986." World Nuclear Association, April 2018. www.world-nuclear.org/information-library/safety-and-security/safety-of-plants/chernobyl-accident.aspx

"Constructing an Argument." Massey University, February 8, 2018. http://owll.massey.ac.nz/study-skills/constructing-an-argument.php

Dlugan, Andrew. "What Is Logos and Why Is It Critical for Speakers?" Six Minutes, August 15, 2010. http://sixminutes.dlugan.com/logos-definition

Dunn, Collin. "Does Recycling Really Make a Difference?" How Stuff Works. https://home.howstuffworks.com/green-living/recycling-difference-green-impact.htm

"Environmental Impacts and Siting of Wind Projects." Office of Energy Efficiency & Renewable Energy. www.energy.gov/eere/wind/environmental-impacts-and-siting-wind-projects

"Examples of Ethos, Logos, and Pathos." Your Dictionary. http://examples.yourdictionary.com/examples-of-ethos-logos-and-pathos.html

"Fukushima Accident." World Nuclear Association, June 2018. www.world-nuclear.org/information-library/safety-and-security/safety-of-plants/fukushima-accident.aspx

Girard, Patrick. "Good and Bad Arguments." Future Learn, University of Auckland. www.futurelearn.com/courses/logical-and-critical-thinking/0/steps/9153

Grabianowski, Ed. "How Recycling Works." How Stuff Works. https://science.howstuffworks.com/environmental/green-science/recycling2.htm

Hutchinson, Alex. "Is Recycling Worth It?" *Popular Mechanics*, November 12, 2008. www.popularmechanics.com/science/environment/a3752/4291566

"Is Recycling Worth It?" *Scientific American*, November 5, 2015. www.scientificamerican.com/article/is-recycling-worth-it

Kellner, Tomas. "How Loud Is A Wind Turbine?" GE Reports, August 2, 2014. www.ge.com/reports/post/92442325225/how-loud-is-a-wind-turbine

Koontz, Robin. "What's Good and What's Bad About Wind Energy." Kids Discover, April 13, 2015. www.kidsdiscover.com/teacherresources/whats-good-whats-bad-wind-energy

Lallanilla, Marc. "Chernobyl: Facts About the Nuclear Disaster." Live Science, September 25, 2013. https://www.livescience.com/39961-chernobyl.html

Lober, Douglas. "How a Landfill Works." Reuse This Bag, March 27, 2018. www.reusethisbag.com/articles/how-a-landfill-works

"Nuclear Energy Pros and Cons." Conserve Energy Future. www.conserve-energy-future.com/pros-and-cons-of-nuclear-energy.php

Parker, Laura. "Ocean Trash: 5.25 Trillion Pieces and Counting, But Big Questions Remain." *National Geographic*, January 11, 2015. http://news.nationalgeographic.com/news/2015/01/150109-oceans-plastic-sea-trash-science-marine-debris

Pyper, Julia. "Does Burning Garbage to Produce Electricity Make Sense?" *Scientific American*, August 26, 2011. www.scientificamerican.com/article/does-burning-garbage-to-produce-energy-make-sense

Ryan, Sheryl. "Which Plastics Can and Cannot Go in the Recycle Bin?" Greenopedia. https://greenopedia.com/plastic-recycling-codes

"The Nuclear Debate." World Nuclear Association, April 2018. www.world-nuclear.org/information-library/current-and-future-generation/the-nuclear-debate.aspx

"Waste Incineration: Advantages and Disadvantages." Greentumble, August 2, 2018. https://greentumble.com/waste-incineration-advantages-and-disadvantages

Weida, Stacey, and Karl Stolley. "Using Rhetorical Devices for Persuasion." Purdue Online Writing Lab, March 11, 2013. https://owl.english.purdue.edu/owl/resource/588/04

"What Is Nuclear Energy." Conserve Energy Future. www.conserve-energy-future.com/disadvantages_nuclearenergy.php

"Wind Turbines Killing More Than Just Local Birds." *Science Daily*, September 29, 2016. www.sciencedaily.com/releases/2016/09/160929143808.htm

Should Clear-Cutting for Agriculture Be Allowed?

Bergeron, Louis. "Most New Farmland Comes from Cutting Tropical Forest, Says Stanford Researcher." *Stanford News*, September 2, 2010. https://news.stanford.edu/news/2010/september/farmland-cutting-forests-090210.html

Bradford, Alina. "Deforestation: Facts, Causes, & Effects." Live Science, April 3, 2018. www.livescience.com/27692-deforestation.html

"Clear-Cutting." Encyclopedia.com. www.encyclopedia.com/environment/energy-government-and-defense-magazines/clear-cutting

"Deforestation." *National Geographic*. www.nationalgeographic.com/environment/global-warming/deforestation

Escobar, Martin, Sandra Uribe, Romina Chiappe, and Cristian Estades. "Effect of Clearcutting Operations on the Survival Rate of a Small Mammal." U.S. National Library of Medicine, National Institutes of Health, March 6, 2015. www.ncbi.nlm.nih.gov/pmc/articles/PMC4352083

"Giant Panda." World Wildlife Fund. www.worldwildlife.org/species/giant-panda

"Habitat Loss." National Wildlife Federation. www.nwf.org/Educational-Resources/Wildlife-Guide/Threats-to-Wildlife/Habitat-Loss

"Harmful Effects of Pesticides on Human Health." Curejoy, February 28, 2018. www.curejoy.com/content/effects-of-pesticides-on-human-health

"Pesticides in Produce Linked with Reduced Fertility in Women." Harvard School for Public Health, 2017. www.hsph.harvard.edu/news/hsph-in-the-news/pesticides-produce-fertility-women

"Regenerating State Forests Takes Planning, Patience." Michigan Government, Department of Natural Resources, September 29, 2016. www.michigan.gov/dnr/0,4570,7-350-79137_79770_79873_80003-394729--,00.html

"Six Benefits of Logging Forests." Future Forest Consulting, February 4, 2016. www.futureforestinc.com/six-benefits-of-logging-forests

"When Is Clearcutting the Right Choice?" Oregon Forests Resources Institute, 2018. https://www.oregonforests.org/clearcutting

Wilber, Hannah. "Get the Scoop on Deforestation in Africa." African Wildlife Foundation, April 22, 2015. www.awf.org/blog/get-scoop-deforestation-africa

Does Bottled Water Do More Harm Than Good?

"Bottled Water Everywhere: Keeping It Safe" U.S. Food and Drug Administration, December 13, 2017. www.fda.gov/forconsumers/consumerupdates/ucm203620.htm

Connell, Molly. "Bottled Water or Tap Water: Pros and Cons for Health and the Environment." Water Benefits Health, 2017. www.waterbenefitshealth.com/bottled-water-or-tap-water.html

"Consumers Prefer Bottled Water." International Bottled Water Association, December 18, 2017. www.bottledwater.org/consumers-prefer-bottled-water-recognize-it-healthy-choice-and-think-it-should-be-available-wherever

"FDA Regulates the Safety of Bottled Water Beverages Including Flavored Water and Nutrient-Added Water Beverages." U.S. Food & Drug Administration, November 15, 2017. www.fda.gov/Food/ResourcesForYou/Consumers/ucm046894.htm

"15 Key Facts and Statistics About Bottled Water." Arcadia Power Blog, 2017. http://powerup.arcadiapower.com/15-key-facts-statistics-bottled-water

"Frequently Asked Questions about Bottled Water." Government of Canada, December 5, 2013. www.canada.ca/en/health-canada/services/food-nutrition/food-safety/information-product/frequently-asked-questions-about-bottled-water.html#a4

Hogan, Chris. "IBWA Bottled Water Industry Update." *Water Conditioning & Purification Magazine,* September 18, 2015. www.wcponline.com/2015/09/18/ibwa-bottled-water-industry-update

"Labeling." International Bottled Water Association. www.bottledwater.org/content/labeling-1

Laville, Sandra, and Matthew Taylor. "A Million Bottles a Minute: World's Plastic Binge 'As Dangerous as Climate Change.'" *The Guardian*, June 28, 2017. www.theguardian.com/environment/2017/jun/28/a-million-a-minute-worlds-plastic-bottle-binge-as-dangerous-as-climate-change

"Pros and Cons of Bottled Water: Is It Good for Your Child?" Smile Center for Kids, July 22, 2017. www.smilecenterforkids.com/blog/pros-cons-bottled-water-good-child

Readfern, Graham. "WHO Launches Health Review After Microplastics Found in 90% Of Bottled Water." *The Guardian*, March 15, 2018. www.theguardian.com/environment/2018/mar/15/microplastics-found-in-more-than-90-of-bottled-water-study-says

Rega, Sam. "Animated Map Shows Where Your Bottled Water Actually Comes From." *Business Insider,* October 20, 2016. www.businessinsider.com/animated-map-bottled-water-springs-dasani-aquafina-2016-10

"*Take Back the Tap*." Food and Water Watch, June 2007. www.countyofkane.org/Recycling/Documents/TakeBackTheTap_web.pdf

"The Bottled Water Industry." Canadian Bottled Water Association. www.cbwa.ca/index.php/about-cbwa/the-bottled-water-industry.html

"24 Bottled Water Statistics." WaterSmart Systems & Plumbing, April 6, 2017. http://watersmartsystems.com/24-Bottled-Water-Statistics.htm

Zeratsky, Katherine. "Is Tap Water as Safe as Bottled Water?" Mayo Clinic. www.mayoclinic.org/healthy-lifestyle/nutrition-and-healthy-eating/expert-answers/tap-vs-bottled-water/faq-20058017

Should Schools Go Paperless?

Adams, Richard. "Students Who Use Digital Devices in Class 'Perform Worse in Exams.'" *The Guardian*, May 11, 2016. www.theguardian.com/education/2016/may/11/students-who-use-digital-devices-in-class-perform-worse-in-exams

"Attention, Students: Put Your Laptops Away." *National Public Radio*, April 17, 2016. www.npr.org/2016/04/17/474525392/attention-students-put-your-laptops-away

"Fun Facts." Paper Recycles. www.paperrecycles.org/about/fun-facts

"Infographic: A Look at the Modern College Student's Use of Technology." Infographics Archive. www.infographicsarchive.com/tech-and-gadgets/a-look-at-the-modern-college-students-use-of-technology

"Is the Paper Industry Getting Greener?" The Conversation, April 26, 2017. http://theconversation.com/is-the-paper-industry-getting-greener-five-questions-answered-76274

Merlin, John. "Is the Paperless School In Sight?" *The Guardian*, January 8, 2008. www.theguardian.com/education/2008/jan/08/link.link2

"Our Industry." American Forest & Paper Association. www.afandpa.org/our-industry/fun-facts

"Paper Use Statistics." Statistic Brain, 2018. www.statisticbrain.com/paper-use-statistics/statisticbrain.com/technology-computers-in

"What Goes Into the Landfill?" Paper Life Cycle. http://thepaperlifecycle.org/end-of-life/in-depth/what-goes-into-the-landfill

GLOSSARY

Please note: Some **boldfaced** words are defined where they appear in the text.

arable Suitable for growing crops
atmosphere The layer of gases surrounding Earth
audience Spectators, listeners, or readers
coniferous Describes a forest made up of evergreen trees that produce cones, for example, pine trees and fir trees, which grow in cooler areas of the world
contaminants Substances that contaminate or pollute something
cosmetics Products applied to the body to improve its appearance
credible Believable or convincing
critical thinking Considering carefully and logically to form a judgment
deforestation Cutting down a large area of forest
detergents Cleaning substances
developing world A term often used by the United Nations and other organizations to describe countries where things such as average income, the strength of the economy, infrastructure such as roads, and poverty, education, and health care are lower or less available in comparison to "developed" countries such as those in Europe and North America
e-books Electronic versions of printed books that can be read on a computer or handheld electronic device
E. coli A type of bacteria that can cause severe food poisoning
economy The prosperity and earnings of a place, such as a country, city, or town
ecosystems Communities of animals and plants and their environment
endangered Describes an animal that is near to extinction
epidemic When a disease affects a large number of people at the same time
evidence Anything, such as data or statistics, that proves or disproves something
export To sell to another country
extinction When no members of a species exist
fertile Able to produce good crops and other plants
fertilizer Chemicals added to soil to increase its fertility for growing plants
fossil fuels Resources such as oil, natural gas, and coal, which formed over millions of years from the remains of dead plants and animals
genders The states of being male or female
generations Groups of people of a similar age to each other
global warming The gradual rise in Earth's temperature caused by greenhouse gases in the atmosphere
greenhouse gases The gases found in Earth's atmosphere that trap heat
herbicides Substances used to kill weeds
hydrated Having enough water to keep healthy
industries Specific types of businesses that make goods or provide services
junk mail Unwanted material received by mail or e-mail
kilowatt hours A unit of energy that is equal to the energy provided by a thousand watts in one hour (a light bulb has a power rating of 25–100 watts)
landfills The places where garbage and other waste material are buried
logging Cutting down trees and preparing the wood for other uses
logic A careful system of thinking and figuring out ideas
managed forests Forests in which at least one tree is planted for every tree felled
mercury A poisonous liquid metal
methane gas A greenhouse gas that is colorless and odorless
municipal Relating to a town or district
noise pollution Harmful or annoying levels of noise
nuclear power Power or energy that comes from nuclear reactions
ore A rock or mineral that contains a useful metal
oxygen A gas that animals and plants need to live and breathe
pediatric occupational therapist A medical professional who helps children recuperate from illness and enables them to perform daily tasks
pesticides Substances used to kill insects that harm plants
plantations Large farms where crops such as coffee and sugar are grown
pollinated When pollen is taken from one plant or part of a plant to another, so that new seeds can be produced
proponents People who speak out in favor of something
pulp Wood fiber used to make paper
radiation The emission of powerful energy
radioactive Giving off energy that is potentially dangerous
renewable Describes resources that will never run out
reservoirs Large lakes used as a source of water supply
resources Things that can be used, such as natural resources, including trees and water, and human-made resources, such as cell phones
soil erosion The wearing away of topsoil by the wind, water, or ice
statistics Facts involving numbers or data
thyroid cancer A disease of the thyroid gland in front of the neck
tinnitus Ringing or buzzing in the ears
toner A chemical used in printers and photocopiers
topsoil The soil closest to the surface that is the most fertile
treated Treated water has had dirt, bacteria, and other contaminants removed to make it safe for drinking
turbines Large wheels with blades that rotate to make electricity
validity Describing something that is sound or well founded
vertigo The sensation of dizziness and loss of balance

LEARNING MORE

Find out more about the arguments concerning the environment.

Books

Doeden, Matt. *Finding Out about Nuclear Energy*. (Searchlight Books, What Are Energy Sources?). Lerner Publishing Group, 2014.

Greene, Carol. *I Love Our Forests*. Enslow Publishing, 2013.

Jakubiak, David J. *What Can We Do About Deforestation?* PowerKids Press, 2011.

Kirk, Ellen. *Human Footprint*. National Geographic Kids, 2011.

Websites

Learn about paperless schools:
www.educationworld.com/a_tech/tech059.shtml

Learn more about writing and evaluating arguments and counterclaims:
www.icivics.org/products/drafting-board

Read more about deforestation:
www.nationalgeographic.com/environment/global-warming/deforestation

Read more about bottled water:
www.scholastic.com/browse/article.jsp?id=3756291

INDEX

agriculture 20, 21, 22, 23, 24, 25, 26
Altamont Pass Wind Resource Area 13
Amazon rain forest 20, 21
American Bird Conservancy 12
arguments 6, 7, 8, 9, 18, 21, 26, 29, 34, 37, 42
atmosphere 5, 38, 39

beaches 35
bees 9
beverages 33
bioplastics 4
bottled water 28, 29, 30, 31, 32, 33, 34, 35

cacao tree 26
cattle ranching 20, 25
chemicals 9, 19, 21, 25, 33
Chernobyl nuclear accident 16
claims 9, 10, 11, 14, 15
clear-cutting 20, 21, 22, 23, 24, 25, 26, 27
clincher 15
conclusion 11, 14, 15
coniferous forests 20
Consumer Reports 32
contaminants 32, 35
core argument 10, 14, 15
counterclaims 11, 14
critical thinking 40, 41, 43

deforestation 4, 5, 23, 24, 27, 36
developing world 20, 23, 26

e-books 38, 42
E. coli 32
economy 22, 25

ecosystems 9, 17, 20, 24, 27, 33
electricity 7, 8, 10, 13
endangered species 13, 24, 25
Environmental Protection Agency (EPA) 18
ethos 16, 17
evidence 8, 9, 11, 14, 15, 31

fertilizers 21, 23, 25, 27
fossil fuels 5, 19, 32

global warming 5
greenhouse gases 18, 19

habitats 24, 25, 27
herbicides 21, 25, 27
Hurricane Katrina 30

industries 4, 5

landfills 4, 6, 7, 18, 19, 29, 32, 33, 38, 39, 42
logging 20, 36
logic 8, 16
logos 16

managed forests 5, 36
Massachusetts Institute of Technology (MIT) 41, 43
mercury 7
methane gas 7, 39, 42
municipal drinking water 32

nearsightedness 40
noise pollution 13
nuclear power 5, 11, 14

paper industry 36, 39
pathos 16
pesticides 21, 23, 25, 27, 28
plantations 22, 25, 26, 27
plastic water bottles 29, 32, 35
power plants 7, 10, 11

recycling 4, 6, 7, 9, 17, 18, 19, 36
red-backed poison frog 27
reservoirs 25, 27
rhetoric 16, 17

solar power 8
statistics 11, 15, 16, 21, 29

tap water 28, 29, 30, 31, 32, 34
technology 37, 39, 40, 41, 43
tropical crops 22, 26
turbines 7, 12, 13

U.S. Food & Drug Administration (FDA) 31

waste food 7
wildlife 12, 13, 21, 23, 24, 25, 32
wind power 5, 13, 14, 15
World Bank 7, 23
World Health Organization (WHO) 16, 32, 35
World Wildlife Fund (WWF) 24, 27

ABOUT THE AUTHOR

Simon Rose is an author of 15 novels and more than 100 nonfiction books. He offers programs for schools, covering the writing process, editing and revision, where ideas come from, character development, historical fiction, story structure, and the publishing world. He is an instructor for adults and offers online workshops and courses. Simon also provides services for writers, including manuscript evaluation, editing, and coaching, plus copywriting services for the business community.